Buddhist

Beginners:

Buddhism Basics, Meditation, Mindfulness Guide For Harmony, Inner Peace, Good Health, Happiness, High Energy Levels, Longevity

By

Brittany Samons

2

Table of Contents

Introduction 5

Chapter 1. Basic Buddhism Principles 6

Chapter 2. Eight Fold Path 10

Chapter 3. Benefits of The Right Understanding 12

Chapter 4. Life Plan 15

Chapter 5. Relaxation 19

Chapter 6. Things That Help Combating Stress and Tension
.... 21

Chapter 7. Five Precepts 23

Chapter 8. Meditation 25

    Meditation Techniques 29

Chapter 9. Buddhism Myths and Misconceptions 32

Conclusion 35

Thank You Page 36

Buddhism For Beginners: Buddhism Basics, Meditation, Mindfulness Guide For Harmony, Inner Peace, Good Health, Happiness, High Energy Levels, Longevity

By Brittany Samons

Introduction

A lot has been said about Buddhism with every scholar trying to understand and portray a scholarly approach to understanding Buddhism. Unfortunately, most of these studies and explanations are not useful especially when needed to serve as a guide of life, which Buddhism should be. Buddhism is a religion based on the teachings of Siddhartha Gautama (Buddha) who is the founder of Buddhism and existed over 25 centuries ago in the northeastern Asian region in today's Nepal.

Buddha means the awakened one due to the experience of profound realizations of the natures of life, death and existence, which are the main principles of Buddhism today. His teachings were on how to realize the same enlighten that he did hence the spread of the belief and religion across Asia and other continents at large. According to Buddha, awakening can only be realized through personal experiences and not through beliefs and dogmas as is often thought of in other religions.

Chapter 1. Basic Buddhism Principles

The only way that human beings can be truly happy, successful and secure is to learn to see the world for what it is and as a result shape activities in line with this understanding. Solutions to problems should be looked for in terms of the cause-effect relationship because the universal law of causality operates in the human behavior field and not the physical world. To have a fruitful life it is important understand the moral law of karma which is a volition action which express moral intentions.

As a result, you should realize that wholesome and unwholesome actions attract good and bad results. This works on the principle that one gets what he or she sows and nothing more or less. The deeds performed in any one life are transferred into our future lives in the form of dispositions/ moods, which explains the cumulative nature of karma. These dispositions usually consist of our life characters traits.

Buddhism is built on the principle of action producing results without the intervention of an external force hence the denial of the existence of a creator-God.

According to these teachings, karma is not fate and neither is it a pre-destination but a willing action that is considered capable of producing results. When the karmic moral law of cause and effect you learn to control our actions in order to serve our own welfare as well as promote the good of others. Buddhism has ten unwholesome courses of actions and deeds whose origin is greed, hatred and delusion defilements. These include lying, slander, killing, stealing, sexual misconduct, useless talk, harsh speech, ill will, covetousness and false views.

Wholesome karma on the other hand comes from the virtuous qualities of wisdom, detachment and good will. They include morality, generosity, reverence and meditation, transference of minds, service, hearing the dhamma, and rejoicing in the good deeds of other, expounding the dhamma and straightening out of one's views. Materialism in the world is triggered by sheer ignorance of the laws of life. When people are convinced that everything perishes, they lose sight of ethical ideas and disregard the consequences of their actions and as such, their life becomes one of pursuit for sensual pleasures. Just as ignorance is no excuse in a court of law, it does excuse you from the, oral karmic laws, there will always be consequences for actions.

Buddhism affirms continuity of life and denies the existence e of a permanent soul. The mind of a dying person due to its craving for continued existence will grasp at some object, idea or person and vitalizes an appropriate life germ. New life forms that germinate are either human or non-human forms. This happens trough a re-birth process that lie latent to previous impressions, characteristics and tendencies of the individual. This means that death leads to birth and the cycles keeps repeating itself. Life problems are resolved by Buddhist middle way, which provides a middle ground between extremes of theism and materialism leading to moral accountability without posing the challenges of positioning a benevolent God. As a result, human beings is a true reflection of their own actions and their evolving is based on the quality of their karma during their lifetime.

There is only way through which we can avoid being unhappy and dissatisfied and that is by eliminating the crave that gives birth to it all. We need to understand that everything sought after ad clung to is impermanent. In addition, nothing, object, experience or person lasts forever. Everything that ruses shall perish and clinging to this will only cause suffering. Eliminating theses carvings is the most difficult part but when we manage to do so we reach an inward state of unshaken calmness and perfection. It is possible to reach the end of our suffering by cultivating the noble eightfold path. This happens in three stages namely morality, concentration and wisdom. Morality will purify conduct whereas concentration makes the mind calm. Due to this wisdom arises and a person is able to have a clear insight and knowledge of things as they are. Wisdom cause all cravings forms to be destroyed forever and the flame of life is extinguished for the want of life. From this, the unconditional is won translating to deathless, bliss and reality.

Chapter 2. Eight Fold Path

The eight components are divided into three categories.

Wisdom group (panna)

This consists of two parts namely the right understanding, which is the knowledge of the true nature of life, and understanding of the four noble truths. The second part is the right though whose focus is on thought that is free from sensuality, ill will and any forms of aggression.

Morality group (sila)

This consist of three parts the first being the right speech that insists on abstinence from falsehood, slander, useless words and harsh speech. The second path, which is the right action focuses on abstinence, form killing, stealing and sexual misconduct. Thirdly, the right livelihood path deals with avoiding any means of livelihood that intends to exploit others.

Concentration group (Samadhi)

The first component is the right effort, which trains the mind to avoid unwholesome mental states and instead work on developing wholesome ones. The second component is the right mindfulness, which is developing power of attentiveness and awareness with regard to the four foundations of mindfulness, which are body, feelings, mind and mental phenomenon. The third component of the Samadhi is the right concentration, which refers to the cultivation of one pointedness of mind.

These eight factors provide a summary of all the teachings of Buddha that one needs to understand to become a true follower. Admiring this way of life is one thing but true commitment is what makes the difference between monks and laymen all of whom start from the same foundation towards a specific goal, nibbana.

Chapter 3. Benefits of The Right Understanding

This is the basis for understanding proper sense of values that prevent dimming and loss of our visions whose result is a misguided and misdirection of plans for individual and social development. When wrong views prevail, we will operate with a perverted sense of values and will be in constant blind pursuit of wealth power and possessions. Right views point us towards an enlightened sense of value that is towards a detachment and kindness, generosity of spirit and selfless service to others and a pursuit for wisdom and understanding. Right livelihood and right action helps in avoiding conflicts that result from a wrong way of life and action.

Having the right understanding also enables one to see that worldly values are manmade and relative. It is these values that lead people astray and causes them to suffer in vain. With Buddhism, you get to learn authentic values which are grounded in timeless truth. The first realization is the true aspects of life, which in turn lead to the reveling if the dharma, which is the external law of righteousness and truth.

The fact that life involves never-ending changes that is subject to many suffering forms, only a person with the right understanding is capable of living a life free of suffering because he or she learns to live simply and regulate the desire. A virtuous person has moderate desires and follows the middle way in all matters. The understanding of the connection between suffering and craving helps home hold back some desires in simple living. A person with the right understanding knows that true happiness is an inward state and quality of mind thus the need to seek it inwardly. The basic physical requirements for sustenance should be wholesome food, shelter, clothing and medicine. Additionally to this should be guarding the doors of sense, right knowledge, virtue and meditation. Living simply leads to contentment and peace of mind, which releases your energy to perform higher virtues and values.

The right understanding is also, what helps Buddhist to stay calm amidst fluctuating life fortunes. You will be able to face calamity without lamentation or falling into despair. Everything that happens to us results from the conditions and cause for which we are ultimately responsible. Understanding the law or karma and re-birth helps master emotional control, which is a major key to happiness. It is safe to say that understanding the same law shows how we are architects of our own destiny.

Understanding also comes with an objective to look at people, things and events objectively, which is a sign of mental maturity. This leads to a saner living and clearer thinking that reduces the susceptibility to wicked influences. The other benefit of right understanding is the ability to think for one self. This involves making important decisions on your own, form personal opinions and face life challenges with formed principles of reality. Finally, the right understanding gives purpose to life. There is an emphasis for a Buddhist in order to have a life full of purpose and worthy aims. To be truly happy there is a need to have a simple but sound life philosophy. This should be a desire to understand the nature of man and our destiny in the universe giving life a meaning and sense of direction. A clear philosophy makes life more fruitful and meaningful, all of which are traits of happiness, which is usually the ultimate goal.

Chapter 4. Life Plan

To realize the full potential of human life there is need to have practical aims to achieve in life. To accomplish this it is needed to have a life plan within the framework of the noble eight fold path. Immediate life aims can be realized by keeping in line with our circumstances and powers. However, makes sure that your life plan is realistic in the sense that it envisions the development of innate potential, which steers us towards realization, and actualization of our possibilities.

The first thing is to have an honest understanding of who we are through self-evaluation and self-examination, which increases the chances of self-improvement. Consider the degree to which you are kind, even-tempered, honest, energetic, truthful, diligent, and industrious, considerate, honest, tolerant, cautious, tactful and patient. It is important to improve areas of weaknesses with a little daily practice. The more an action is performed the easier it gets and with time, it becomes a habit that is ingrained in our character. A good life plan should cover all areas of normal household life including marriage, occupation, procreation and raising children, retirement, old age and death.

Obstacles and challenges

Several things towards achieving what they seek when choosing the right path hinder Buddhist. They are known as the five mental hindrances. Because of the fact that they close the doors to both spiritual and worldly progress. They were originally taught as the hindrances to meditation but are also applicable in general life success achievement.

Sensual craving

This being the first hindrance refers to the obsessive yearning for possessions or sense gratification. This does not mean that a Buddhists should not seek wealth and possession as an ultimate happiness goal, it only means that there must be an understanding of its limits. Here is the understanding that unfair acquisition of power and wealth coupled with a strong attachment to them can only lead to misery and despair instead of joy and contentment. Failure to understand this will lead to signs of insecurity which manifest in an extreme desire for sex enjoyment, liquor and riches all of which must be avoided,

Ill will or hatred

This is the second hindrance that is the emotional opposite equal of desire. It is a potent obstacle for progress. Like and dislike are both forces that can trigger conflicts and bloodshed because of the confusion, both are born out of ignorance. While desire drives us to get what we want, hatred colors everything black and pushes us to destroy anything that is suspected to be hostile to our interests.

Indolence and mental inertia

This hindrance is an obstacle to strenuous effort. Lazy people are not inclined to strive for correct understanding of high conduct standards. Due to this nature, he becomes an easy prey to craving and desires.

Restlessness and worry

This twin hindrances are common in today's world. Restlessness is manifest in the agitation, impatience, and thirst of excitement and unsettled character of daily living. Worry on the other hand is a guilt and remorse feeling that broods sadly and regrettably over an evil deed done or good deed left undone. The best remedy for what has been done is a conscious choice to do it again whereas the remedy for neglect is to take action immediately.

Doubt

This is the last hindrance, which refers to the inability to decide or a lack of resolution that prevents one from making a firm commitment to higher ideals and pursuance of good with a steady will. If not contained these five hindrances come in the way of one's progress and deprive the mind of understanding and happiness. However, with the cultivation of cardinal virtues which are confidence, energy, mindfulness, concentration and wisdom.

Chapter 5. Relaxation

Relaxation is a necessary component for happiness especially in the modern life, which is full of stress. It is possible to exist calmly amidst strenuous conditions by understanding its causes and how best they can be minimized. While hard work never killed anyone, people work anxiously because they are driven by an intense desire and craving. Common scenarios are where people are so driven that they cannot rest until the goal is achieve or they are filled with fear of losing the price that they decide not to relax and enjoy. In certain cases, there is the resentment towards persons or things that try to deter one from their goal and others are on the constant hanker for power, position or prestige all at the expense of others.

In order to avoid stress or strain it is important to train the mind to envision persons, encounters, experiences and objects realistically as transient phenomenon. There is need to reflect upon them in three characteristics which are impermanent, unsatisfactorily and without self. Doing this will reduce the investment you make on self-concern which in turn lovers the crave and desire attachment. Avoid anger, pride and anxiety and selfish thoughts that prioritize "me" as this are the emotions that lead to strain and stress.

Chapter 6. Things That Help Combating Stress and Tension

Keeping the five precepts of conscientiously

The feeling of guilt is to increase stress and by observing the precepts you will be able to have a life that is a blameless life and enjoy freedom from a nagging sense of guilt which in the rules of basic in their morality is damaging.

Sense of control

The mind is constantly attracted to pleasant sense objects and replied by unpleasant ones. Reckless wandering therefore causes distraught and scattering. Your mind will then become settled and calm as well and after this you will get a result of and experience and a happiness that is unblemished.

Meditation

Meditation is the best way to purify the mind. As the mind is gradually, cleansed one can see with greater clarity the true nature of life. Person becomes more and more detached from worldly things and develops a composure that can't be shaken even with the changes that brings life.

Cultivating the four sublime attitudes

These attitudes include kindness, compassion, joy and composure. These enlightened emotions reduce the stress of daily living. This improves your interpersonal relationships at home and at the workplace. This helps in the development of an even mind, which increases calmness and inner peace.

Chapter 7. Five Precepts

This is the code of ethics that any lay Buddhist should follow. Those are moral rules voluntarily undertaken to promote personal conduct purity and staying away from doing harm and suffering to other beings. Evil conduct not only harms oneself and others but also strengthens vices such as greed, hatred and delusion. Engaging in unwholesome conduct violates the cosmic moral law that causes suffering both in life and future existence. The five precepts are as follows:

To abstain from killing living beings

To abstain from taking what is not given

To stay away from sexual misconduct

To abstain from false speech

To abstain from intoxicants and harmful drugs

If you follow the precepts also means that you shun from five kind of occupation forbidden by Buddhist. It forbids trading in arms, human beings, in flesh, in intoxicants and in poisons. Observing these precepts thoroughly in daily living brings about a simultaneous growth in mental purity, skillfulness, and wisdom. A good example is when one refrains from killing it increases compassion and loving kindness for all living beings. The habitual practice of these precepts increases self-control and strength of character any mind that succeeds in controlling desire even to the smallest extent gains power. When desire is uncontrolled, it expends it pursuit to harmful things. The Buddha teaching does not encourage the production of desire but instead counsels on the best way to harness, divert, sublimate or use it in worthwhile causes.

Chapter 8. Meditation

Most things in life may be beyond our control. Even so, it is still possible to take care of our own states of mind, which helps them to change for the better. Buddhism teaches that achieving this state is the most important thing as it is the antidote for many life problems; meditation is a form of transforming the mind. The practices and the techniques of the meditation used encourage and your concentration will develop, the emotional and positivity clarity which help with seeing things in a clam nature. Through engaging with some of the practice of meditation, you learn the habits and patterns of your mind and you will get offers a means of cultivating new and positive ways of being.

Meditation of the Buddhist known to be the concentration of the mind that leads to ultimately spiritual and enlighten freedom. It has developed characteristic variations in different Buddhist variations. There are two types of variations namely the insight and tranquility. The two are used in combination or alternately to achieve desired results.

The main purpose of this meditation techniques s to steal the mind and train it to concentrate.

Tranquility meditation/ Samantha

The goal of this meditation is to progress through its four stages or dhyanas. These stages include the following:

Detachment from external world and consciousness of joy and tranquility

Concentration with suppression of reasoning and investigation

passing away of joy but with the sense of tranquility remaining

the passing away of tranquility and also brings about state of pure self-possession and composure

Insight meditation/ Vipassana

Many of the skills learnt in tranquility meditation can be used in insight meditation but the end goals are different. The purpose of insight meditation is to realize important truths. The person that practices this type of meditation seeks to realize truths of impermanence, suffering and the no-self state. Even though as a Buddhist you probably know the basics about these teachings you need to focus on the object of concentration in an almost trance like manner.

Gaining the skill of mindfulness is the first step of insight meditation. The most common methods that can help develop the necessary mindfulness you should develop walking mindfulness, sitting mindfulness and mindfulness of daily activities.

Walking mindfulness is a common practice in monasteries and retreats especially in Theravada tradition. You can also practice the same as long as you find a quiet place to walk, take relaxation moments and attempt to focus on a myriad of movements and sensation associated with walking. Buddhist practicing this type of meditation say that it gets easier as one progresses in skill and loses oneself. This is blissful in itself but also brings the practitioner closer to insight into the fundamental truths of no self and impermanence.

Sitting mediation is similar to walking meditation only that the focus is on the breathing and not walking. The sitting meditator focuses on his or her breathe as it moves in and out. Just like in walking meditation, as other thoughts distract they should be mindfully recognized and set aside. With practice, the meditator gets less distracted.

Meditation Techniques

The sitting meditation stance (15 to 30 minutes for beginners)

This is what most of the other meditation techniques base on. Find yourself a soft cushion or pillow to sit on. You could use the meditation pillows, the zafus and zabutons. For beginners, finding an absolutely quiet room will make the process easier. Sit down on the mat or cushion probably cross-legged as this is the most common style preferred by most people. You can also kneel on the cushion with your bottom on your feet. When stating out the lotus position should not worry you as it requires time.

Rest on your lap with the palms facing upwards. Close your eyes and start counting your breathes with an emphasis being on deep and slow breathes. Sometimes you may miss the counts but this should not worry you. Every exhalation you will feel your tension going out. When thoughts get out of your mind, you should not try to follow them. Keep on increasing the meditation time as you get a better hang of it. Doing it twice a week in a spaced out manner (four days between schedules is enough)

Concentration meditation (20 to 40 minutes)

This is all about focusing on one thing. It could be a spot at the distance, your breath or something on your mind. Take a candle and place it in front of you then stare at it. Alternatively, you can count beads on the rosary. This type of meditation increases your power to ignore distractions and focus you mind onto one thing. It increases your overall concentration power in real life

You can increase the time span as you advance in your meditation prowess. Since it takes less time, you can do it more times in a week. Do it whenever you can before going to bed or after waking up.

Mindful meditation (15 to 45 minutes)

Other than letting wandering thoughts go, this technique focuses on tracking them as they drift along in your mind. The goal is to be aware of the thoughts as they stem but not to be involved in finding out more about them. This makes you a passive observer of your brain.

Get a stance, most probably the sitting meditation stance and calm yourself. Don't force your brain to see the wandering thought. Just relax until they begin to appear. After this, just note them and their patters. For instance, you can note that you hate papaws, only don't try to find out why you do. That is the core essence of mindful meditation

Mindful meditation is tricky. You will need a lot of practice to make it to 60 minutes. The more you can do it the better. This should be a daily meditation feature. You can do it up to seven times in a day provided you can still your mind well enough. After the session, you will feel better even if you did it on the bas or at work.

Chapter 9. Buddhism Myths and Misconceptions

Like any other religion, there are loads of misconceptions and myths shrouding the true concept of Buddhism. In search for the truth, these will prove to be huge stumbling stones that could either guide you out of the way or make you dislike the religion for nothing. To ensure that you have the right information on Buddhism, we have taken the time to clarify on the most common myths to ensure you have nothing but the truth.

Buddha was a god

Many people, both followers and none followers, think that Buddha was a god. He wasn't a god. He even insists that he is no god but a man just got enlightened out of his own personal hard work.

Buddhism worships a god

This is the skewed truth. Buddhism is all about following a path, not anyone. Since it is all about doing what is right, sensible and helpful to humanity nature and the environment, Buddhism could easily pass as a philosophy rather than as a religion.

Buddhism and meat

Most people believe that Buddhists cannot consume meat. While most are vegetarians out of a misunderstanding, the most enlightened know that Buddha philosophy allowed eating meat provided you did not see the animal die or it was not killed for you. To them, they stick to vegetarian diets as they are healthier.

Buddhism and suffering

Buddhism does not welcome or rejoice at suffering. You do not have to suffer to conform. The ideal is embracing it and taking it positively. In this way, you will grumble less and leave your brain free to chart the best course out of your predicament.

Meditation

Buddhist monks are known to meditate for long in quest for enlightenment. With this in mind, most people think that you must spend hours of strenuous meditation to conform as a Buddhist. This is not mandatory. Things only get tough as you search for greater levels of enlightenment.

Conclusion

To follow any school of thought diligently, you must be both devoted and willing to conform to its most basic facts. Your willingness and devotion to Buddhism should be your only fuel to enlightenment. With Buddhism focused on making you a better person, both in the eyes of the society and for your own sake, applying it in your daily life should not be a problem at all. Since there is the option of learning the religion on your own, you can subscribe to online classes or search for material needed to follow all the elements of the path to enlightenment.

Of most importance to beginners and people seeking to live in accordance with the principles without necessarily reaching total enlightenment, living by the five precepts would be a good place to begin from. Ideally, you should observe all of them. However, depending on the sect of Buddhism you subscribe to, you can get the edge of a couple. Moreover, since it is all about a path, you can always choose to live with what you must and avoid the ones that lead to higher enlightenment only monks seek.

Thank You Page

I want to personally thank you for reading my book. I hope you found information in this book useful and I would be very grateful if you could leave your honest review about this book. I certainly want to thank you in advance for doing this.

If you have the time, you can check my other books too.

Lightning Source UK Ltd.
Milton Keynes UK
UKHW021447160420
361797UK00008B/1666

9 781681 859361